MODERN READING TEXT *in* 4/4

By **LOUIS BELLSON**
Written in Collaboration with
GIL BREINES

FOR ALL INSTRUMENTS

Contents

LOUIS BELLSON

The musical facts about Louis Bellson are indeed amazing. His laurel-winning drumming for Benny Goodman, Tommy Dorsey, Count Basie, and Duke Ellington are permanently etched in recordings and transcriptions.

His unusual talent as an arranger, composer, and conductor are well known in both the jazz and legitimate field.

His ability as a lecturer and percussion clinician is highly regarded among music educators as well as professional musicians, teachers, and students.

The contributions that Louis Bellson has made and is continuing to make to music and percussion will long be remembered.

GIL BREINES

Gil Breines studied percussion with Fred Albright, Saul Goodman, and Morris Goldenberg.

He has a Bachelor of Science Degree from Juilliard School of Music, N. Y., and a Masters Degree from Roosevelt University, Chicago.

He was principal percussionist with the Chicago Symphony Orchestra, and also played with the New York Philharmonic Orchestra, Metropolitan Opera Orchestra and the Goldman Band.

Mr. Breines has performed with such great conductors as Fritz Reiner, Leonard Bernstein, Eugene Ormandy, Leopold Stokowski, Sir Thomas Beechman, Franz Allers, Robert Russel Bennet, Morton Gould among others.

He was on the faculty of the American Conservatory of Music, Chicago, and is now engaged in free lance work in Radio, T.V., and Recordings, as well as being actively engaged in teaching in New York City.

PREFACE

SYNCOPATION=*definition*=Play by accenting notes normally unaccented.

A more understandable definition of syncopation is where the original rhythm or part of a melody or main theme is transferred from the main beats in a measure to "off beat" rhythms. Thus the main melody or theme is still preserved, but more interesting rhythms are created with the melody.

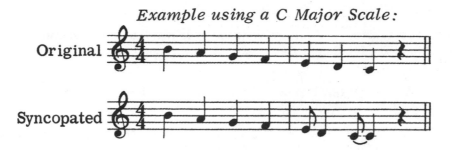

Example using a C Major Scale:

Notice the change in the melody just by changing the last three notes.

The object of this text is to acquaint the reading Musician with the most comprehensive and popular methods of notating syncopated rhythms used in all forms of music. *(ie; Jazz, Classical, Latin, Show, Dance Bands, etc.)*

The speed of the exercises is determined by the ability of the student. In the beginning everything should be played slowly, until the ability to read in an even tempo is ob - tained. The exercise should be played only as fast as the hardest measure of the exercise can be played.

It is suggested by the authors that each rhythmic figure that presents a problem be thoroughly understood. This can be accomplished by first analizing the Rhythmic Figure, and then developing the ability to recognize the Rhythmic Figure. After thoroughly understanding and really knowing the figure you can progress to the next problem.

The art of being able to "Break Down" and then having the ability to recognize a Rhythmic Figure are the two requirements needed in improving ones speed and accuracy in sight reading.

Counting is a must in order to divide the music correctly into its rhythmic sequence. Before leaving a study you should be able to read the entire study smoothly with equal volume throughout and in strict tempo.

In order to get the most out of this text it is suggested by the authors that the music be played both in 4/4 time (C) (making sure you COUNT IN FOUR and BEAT YOUR FOOT IN FOUR) and also in 2/2 time (¢) (making sure that you COUNT IN TWO and BEAT YOUR FOOT IN TWO).

In order to become fully acquainted with reading of modern syncopation, the student must learn to play the exercises not only legitimately, exactly as written, but also with a "Jazz Feel".

This is accomplished by playing all notes that fall on the second half of a quarter note on the third eighth of a triplet, and the 16th note of a dotted 8th and 16th on the third eighth of a triplet.

Example:

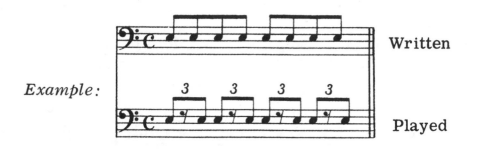

Written

Played

An eighth and sixteenth can be interpreted this way too:

Example:

Written

Played

An example combining all:

Example:

Written

Played

When first practicing in the "Jazz Feel", the student should beat his foot in four.

A good example of the "Jazz Feel" can be seen by comparing the 1st exercise in this book with the exercise on Page 48. This is how the 1st exercise would be played with a "Jazz Feel".

INTRODUCING QUARTER NOTES, EIGHTH NOTES, EIGHTH RESTS

Summary:

Summary:

6

Summary:

COMPLETE SUMMARY OF PAGES FOUR THROUGH SEVEN

INTRODUCING THE TIE

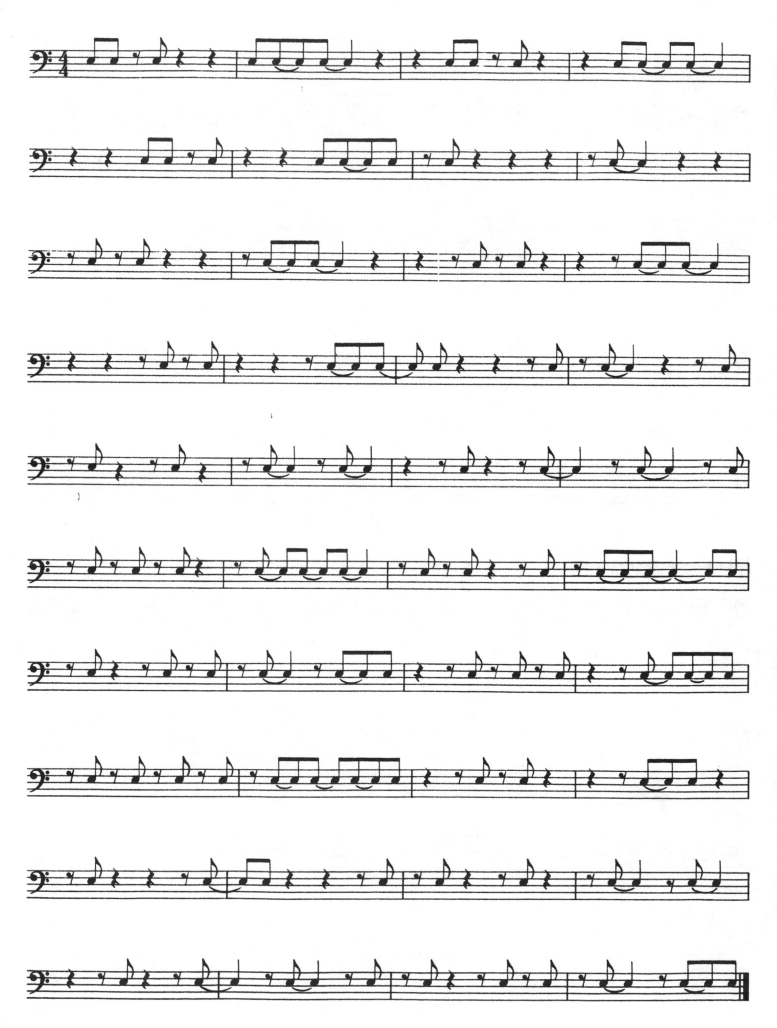

INTRODUCING DOTTED NOTES AND RESTS

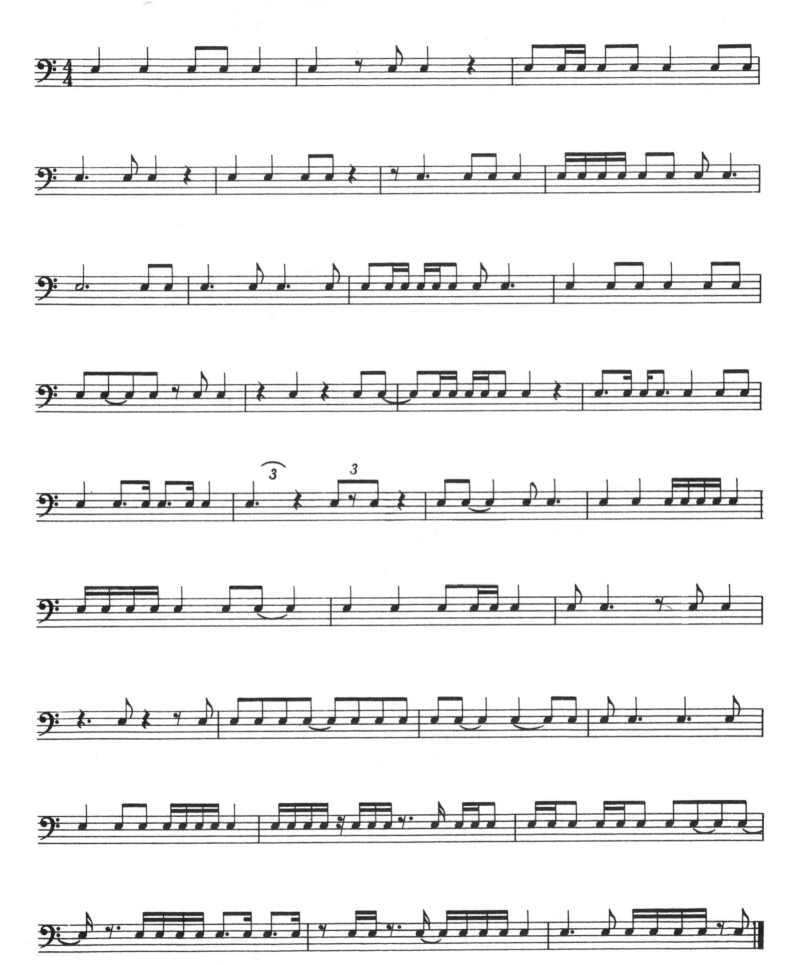

COMMON WRITING OF SYNCOPATION

EXERCISE USING RESTS

TEN SYNCOPATED EXERCISES

18

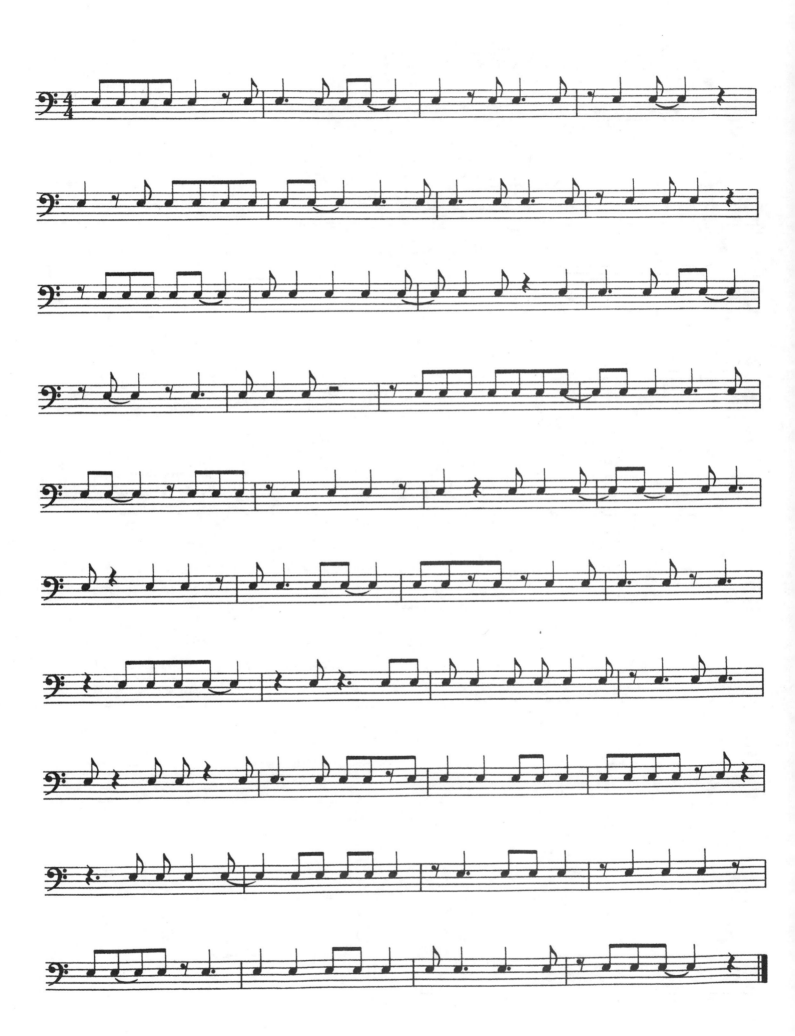

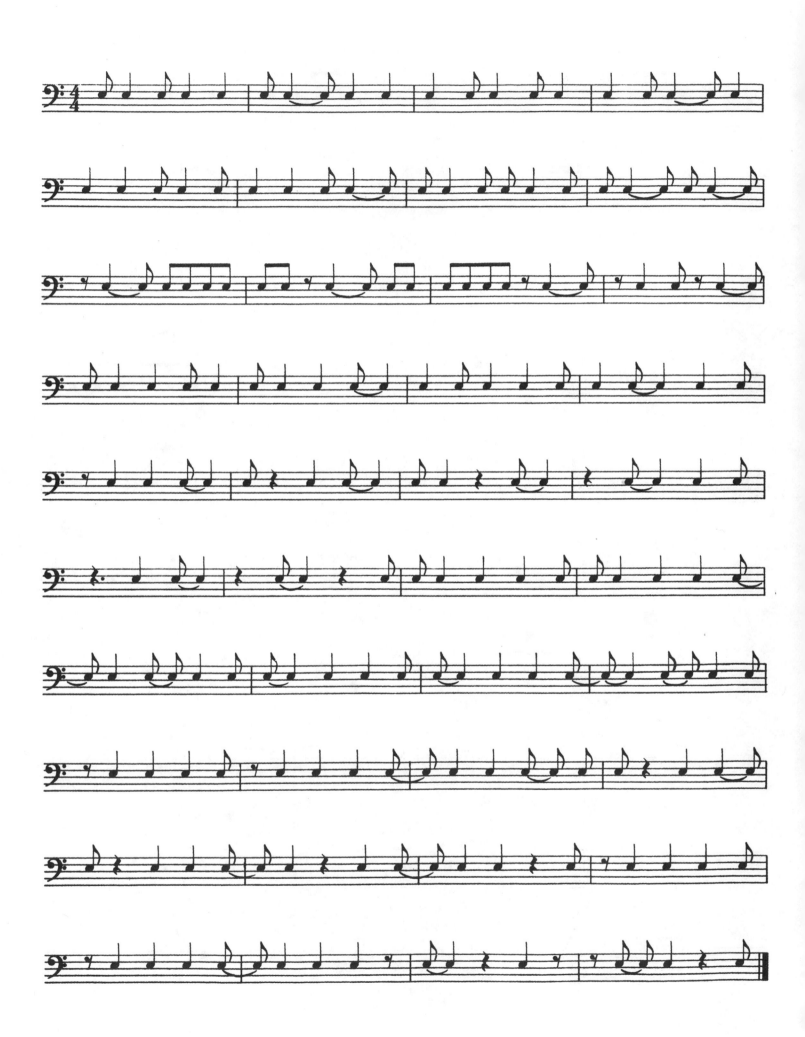

INTRODUCING SIXTEENTH NOTES AND SIXTEENTH RESTS

30

INTRODUCING SIXTEENTH NOTE TIES

34

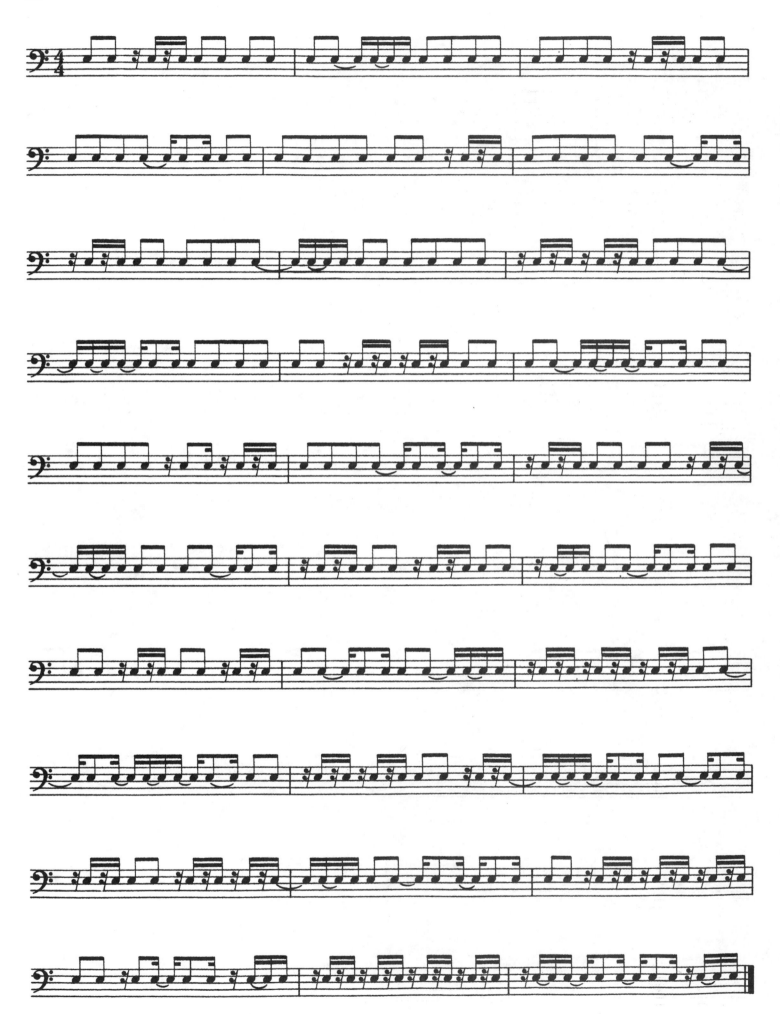

SUMMARY OF PAGES THIRTY-TWO THROUGH THIRTY-EIGHT

TEN SYNCOPATED EXERCISES WITH SIXTEENTH NOTES

44

INTRODUCING EIGHTH NOTE TRIPLETS
(Having the value of a Quarter Note or its equivalent)

49

INTRODUCING EIGHTH NOTE TRIPLETS
(With Sixteenth Notes and Sixteenth Rests)

TRIPLETS USING TIES

TRIPLET TIES AND SIXTEENTH NOTES

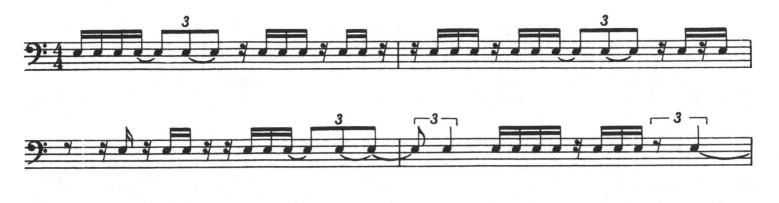

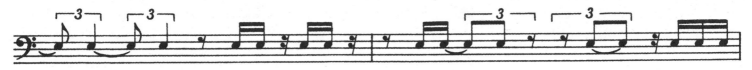

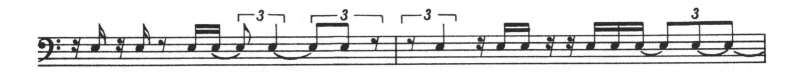

60

INTRODUCING THE QUARTER NOTE TRIPLET

(Having the value of a Half Note or its equivalent)

ADDING SIXTEENTH NOTES

INTRODUCING HALF NOTE TRIPLETS
(Having the value of a Whole Note or its equivalent)

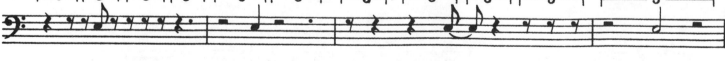

SYNCOPATION WITH TRIPLETS

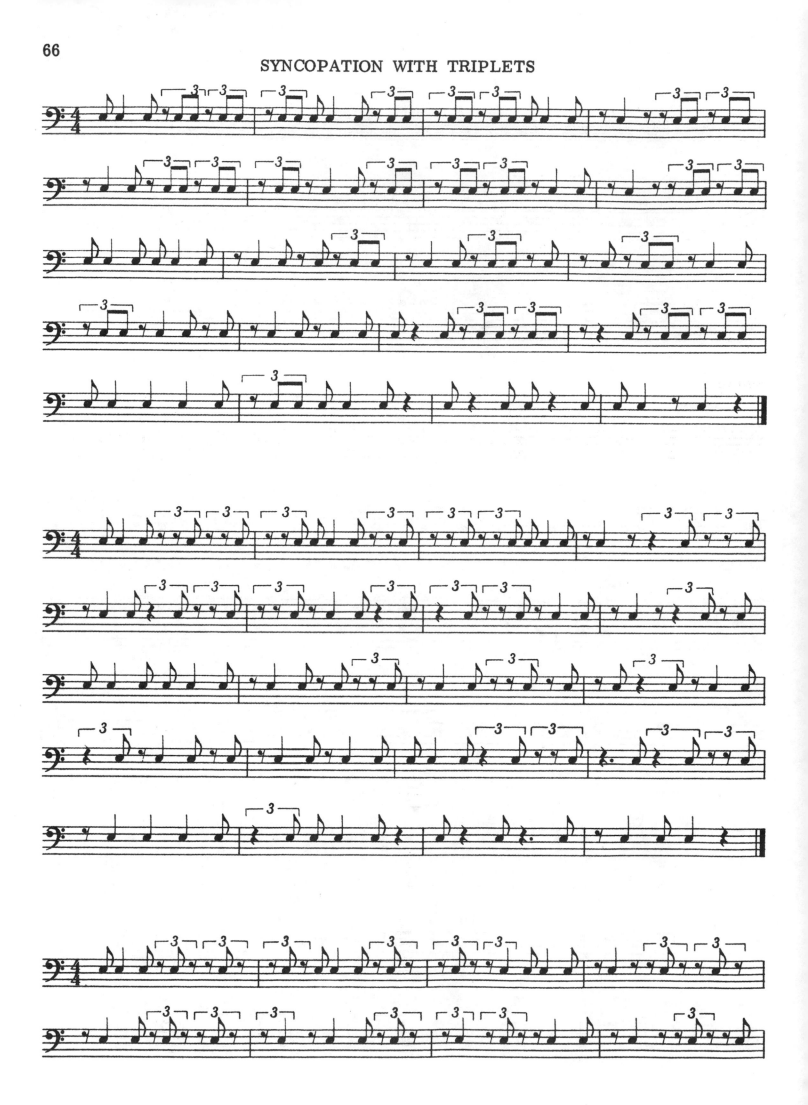

Summary:

FOURTEEN EXERCISES

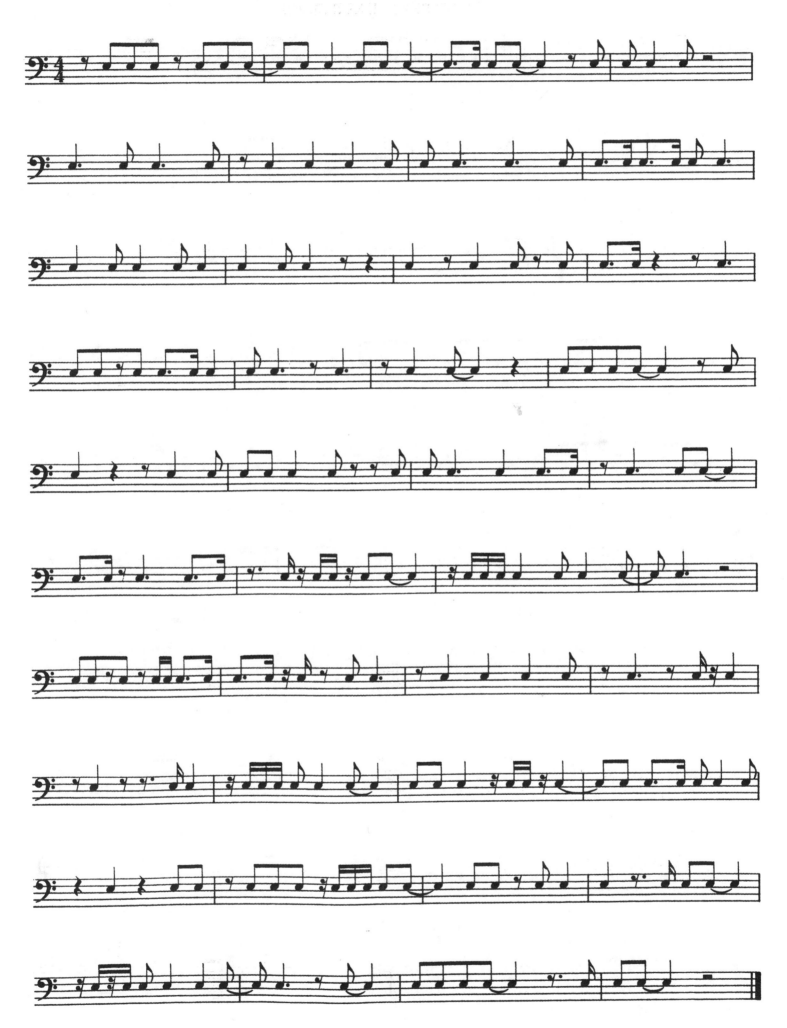

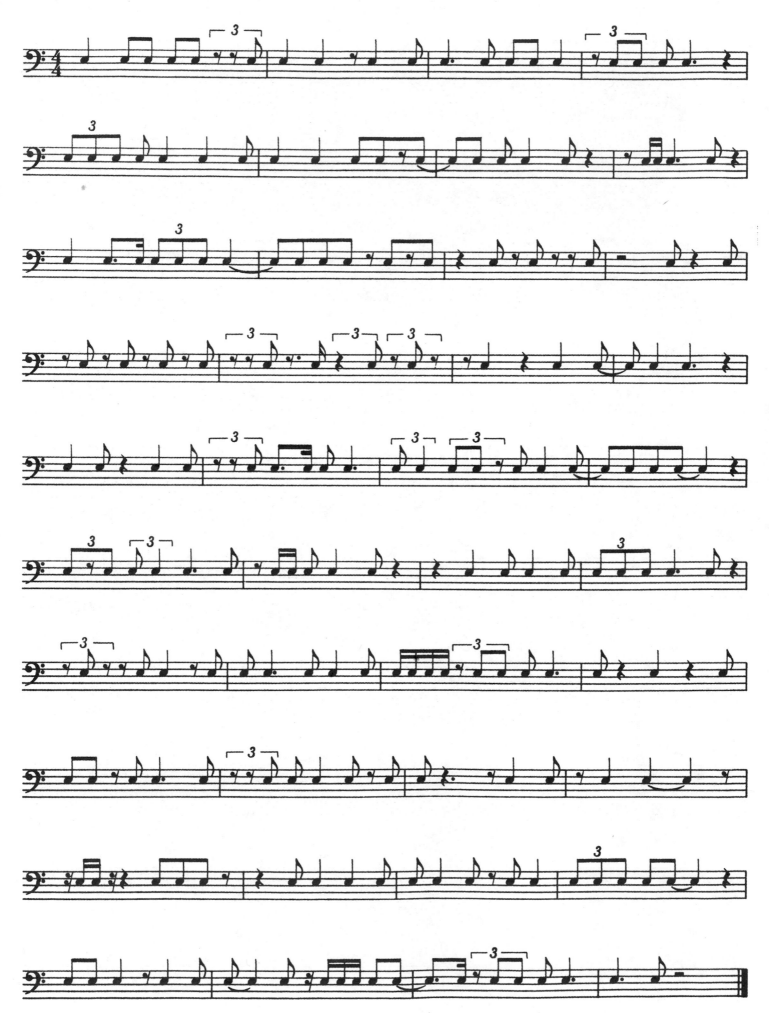

INTRODUCING SIXTEENTH NOTE TRIPLETS
(Having the value of an Eighth Note or its equivalent)

INTRODUCING THIRTY-SECOND NOTES
(Having the value of an Eighth Note or its equivalent)

TWO EXERCISES

INTRODUCING DOUBLE TIME

1. Practice each line separately.
2. Combine all lines as one study.

1. Practice each line separately.
2. Combine all lines as one study.

TWO MEASURE DOUBLE TIME PHRASES

1. Practice each line separately.
2. Combine all lines as one study.

THREE EXERCISES

ATTENTION ALL DRUMMERS

Introducing The *Savage* Rudimental Workshop!

Savage Rudimental Workshop
by Matt Savage
(0465B)

The *Savage Rudimental Workshop* is a state-of-the-art resource for developing total control of the 40 Percussive Arts Society rudiments in a musical context with immediate results.

- The beginning student will discover the basic workings of the essential rudiments.

- The intermediate student will apply the rudiments in more complex ways.

- The advanced student will take the rudiments to higher levels of understanding, composition, and performance.

The book is made up of three components:

RUDIMENT EXERCISES — Each rudiment includes a collection of short exercises, allowing the player to understand how each rudiment is put together and how it can be played in the most efficient and controlled manner.

RUDIMENT SOLOS — Each rudiment includes a solo using the particular skills learned. Each incorporates dynamics, sticking patterns, and phrasing and gradually increases in difficulty from beginning to end, allowing players of all levels to be challenged at different points throughout the solo.

COMPACT DISCS — The two CDs include selected exercises with the rudiment solo and accompaniment for each and ten groove tracks for use with the exercises that offer a number of different tempos, styles, and feels to encourage musicality and groove. The CDs also enable the player to choose to listen to the solo material, the accompaniment, or both at the same time by adjusting the balance on the stereo.

Percussion Books from Warner Bros. Publications

Conversations in Clave
(The Ultimate Technical Study of Four-Way Independence in Afro-Cuban Rhythms)
by Horacio "El Negro" Hernandez
(0444B) Book and CD

This detailed and methodical approach will develop four-limb coordination and expand rhythmic vocabulary. Understanding clave and the relationship between eighth-note and triplet rhythms will aid in mastering the multiple and complex rhythms of Afro-Cuban styles. Stylistic groove transcriptions include Cascara, Guaguanco, Mambo, Macuta, Songo, and Mozambique.

The Drum Set Crash Course
by Russ Miller
(PERC9611CD) Book and CD

This book covers the essential foundations and grooves that will prepare the drummer for a variety of musical situations encountered on the average professional gig. Designed to be an encyclopedia of many drumming styles, *The Drum Set Crash Course* covers Afro-Cuban, Brazilian, blues, country, hip-hop, jazz, reggae, rock, and much more.

Extreme Interdependence
(Drumming Beyond Independence)
by Marco Minnemann, written in collaboration with Rick Gratton
(0560B) Book and CD

Cutting-edge techniques to master four-limb independence from German drum sensation Marco Minnemann. His method will dramatically increase independence and coordination skills and help develop facility on the drum set in all styles. Included are patterns, melodies for two limbs, extreme hi-hat and flam techniques, extreme soloing and independence grooves, and more. A bonus section includes play-along material from Marco's solo CDs and actual workshop sheets from his amazing clinics. Interdependence: the ability to switch any pattern to any limb at any time—complete freedom!

Jungle/Drum 'n' Bass for the Acoustic Drum Set
(A Guide to Applying Today's Electronic Music to the Drum Set)
by Johnny Rabb
(0570B) Book and Two CDs

This book and two-CD package is a must for all drummers wanting to explore the world of electronically produced jungle/drum 'n' bass grooves! If you are new to jungle, it will open the door to new grooves, loops, and sounds on the acoustic drum set. It also provides a wealth of exercises, transcriptions, and sound applications to achieve the feel and style of these futuristic beats. The two CDs include exercise examples from each chapter, basic electronics, and seven original play-along groove loops.

Rhythmic Illusions
by Gavin Harrison
(EL9655CD) Book and CD

Created for drum set players who find themselves in a creative rut, this book and audio package easily breaks down the mystery behind subdivisions, rhythmic modulation, rhythmic scales, and beat displacement. The author makes the transition from mathematics to musicality in an easy and systematic approach.

Rhythmic Perspectives
by Gavin Harrison
(0425B) Book and CD

Rhythmic Perspectives is a book that covers cutting-edge drum concepts and offers mind-expanding exercises to further develop the study of rhythmic illusions and multidimensional rhythm. These concepts are "mind rudiments" for a unique way of thinking about rhythmic structure, rhythmic composition, and higher rhythmic awareness.

Printed in USA   AD1054

THE DRUM SET CRASH COURSE

Russ Miller's Drum Set Crash Course "System" consists of three books and one video, **The Drum Set Crash Course, Transitions, The Crash Course Play-Along,** and **The Drum Set Crash Course** video. Though each book and video work independently of each other, the student gains the most by using the complete system.

Full live-band play-along CDs with all books

"**THE DRUM SET CRASH COURSE** system was introduced in 1997. Its basic concept is to introduce the student to many different musical styles, achieved by analyzing the foundations of more than 18 styles of music, practicing what is required to perform each style effectively, and performing with the CD play-alongs to emphasize the overall musicality of the student's talents. This new methodical and musical approach to learning the art of drumming has been accepted with an enthusiastic response from educators, students, and publications around the world."

— Russ Miller

Russ Miller

Considered a top session and touring drummer, Russ demonstrates his approach to learning *music,* which has allowed him to work with more than 20 of today's biggest stars as well as performing on hundreds of CDs and international movie soundtracks. This video is a wealth of information and insight from one of today's most prominent drummers!

TRANSITIONS
0418B
(Book and CD)

TRANSITIONS is designed to be the first step of the *Crash Course* system. Its focus is on the physical development needed to execute all of these different musical styles and is one of the most complete independence learning systems available. Maintaining the *Crash Course* system's emphasis on musicality, *Transitions* uses full live-band play-alongs for each independence exercise throughout the book.

THE DRUM SET CRASH COURSE book and DVD encapsulates the entire *Crash Course* system. Starting with the physical considerations covered in *Transitions* and continuing with in-depth studies of more than 18 different styles of music, which include rock, jazz, fusion, funk, hip-hop, second-line, Afro-Cuban, Brazilian, country, reggae, and many more! This DVD is the most comprehensive all-in-one drum set learning tool available.

THE DRUM SET CRASH COURSE
PERC9611CD
(Book and CD)

THE DRUM SET CRASH COURSE
904497 (DVD)

Coming soon from Russ Miller: **THE DRUM SET CRASH COURSE PLAY-ALONG PACKAGE** will include all of the songs featured in the video with Russ playing and a remix without drums so you can practice, as well as some of the key grooves and exercises from the video.

All 3 titles have been voted #1 Educational Books and Video Modern Drummer Readers' Poll 2001–2002

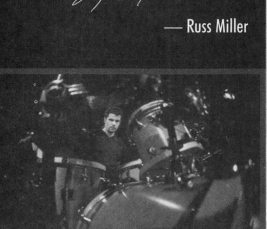

THE DRUM SET CRASH COURSE *succeeds where many other drum books fail! This is a model for all basic drum books to follow!* **DRUMMER**